KU-621-215

Historic IRELAND

Benbulben Mountain

Historic
IRELAND

5,000 YEARS OF IRELAND'S HERITAGE

Dáithí Ó hÓgáin

GILL & MACMILLAN

Skellig Michael

Originally published by Salamander Books Limited 2001

Published in Ireland by
Gill & Macmillan Ltd., Hume Avenue, Park West, Dublin 12
with associated companies throughout the world
www.gillmacmillan.ie

copyright © Salamander Books Limited, 2001

All rights reserved. Except for use in a review, no part of this book may be reproduced, stored in a retrieval system or transmitted in any form or by any means, electronic, mechanical, photocopying or otherwise, without prior written permission from the copyright owner and Publisher.

All correspondence concerning the content of this volume should be addressed to Salamander Books Ltd.

ISBN 0-7171-3256-0

The Author

Dáithí Ó hÓgáin, MA, PhD, is Associate Professor at University College, Dublin, where he lectures on Irish folklore. He is the author of more than 20 books, many of them in Irish, on aspects of folk culture and tradition, and these include books of poetry and short stories. He is a well-known conference lecturer, has participated in the production of documentary films in Europe and the United States, and is a frequent radio and TV broadcaster.

Credits

Project Manager: Ray Bonds
Designers: Interprep Ltd.
Picture researcher: Brian Kelly
Colour reproduction: Studio Tec
Printed and bound in Italy

The Rock of Cashel

Croagh Patrick

Contents

Introduction

Long ago in Ireland, in the area of east Ulster, there lived a young prince called Mongán, who was gifted by nature with great intelligence. His father, the local king Fiachna, was anxious to increase the prestige of his realm. To this end, Fiachna invited the chief-poet of Ireland, Eochaidh, to be his guest, and Mongán was warned not to be impertinent to the distinguished visitor. Soon after the arrival of Eochaidh, however, Mongán disguised himself and contrived to meet the visitor at three different locations, a standing-stone, the ruins of an ancient dwelling, and a tumulus. He asked Eochaidh to tell the history of these three remains, and on each occasion the great man had no choice but to invent a story. Mongán then related the true history of each. Recognising that the disguised youth was in fact the son of his host, Eochaidh flew into a rage and cursed the youth.

The chief-poet in that story was embarrassed because he had been shown to be deficient in his art, for poets were the leading caste of learned men and should have full knowledge of the history of the landscape. That history was known as *seanchas* ('old lore'), and was held in such high regard because it brought the people into a special relationship with their habitat. Mongán and Eochaidh lived in the 7th century AD, and in later mediaeval times a whole series of short texts was compiled on the

Jerpoint Abbey

dinnseanchas ('old place-lore') of Ireland. These texts encapsulated the traditions associated with every notable feature of the countryside, whether natural or cultural. They are not, of course, entirely reliable, for when the mediaeval scholars – like Eochaidh – were at their wit's end to explain something they resorted to fiction.

This volume of illustrations deals with sixty of Ireland's most celebrated places and things, and we are fortunate to have a somewhat richer array of sources than was available to the wise men of old. These sources range from archaeology to written history, and from literature to popular legend. Together with the magnificent photographs, it is hoped that the volume will serve as a modern handbook of *dinnseanchas*. The reader may, of course, decide to undertake an actual 'circuit' or tour of Ireland, as the ancient poets often did, and in that case the volume should serve as an inspiring introduction and guide. The greatest satisfaction is always gained when the visitor not only sees and examines the objects but also gets an insight into their history and meaning, into that whole poetic complex which imbues one with a sense of atmosphere. We extend an invitation to a creative involvement with some of the finest representations of Irish history and culture.

– Dáithí Ó hÓgáin

Powerscourt Demesne

CONNACHT

*Benbulben mountain,
County Sligo*

Dún Aonghusa
County Galway

This great 'fortress of Aonghus' on Inishmore, the largest of the Aran Islands, is situated on the edge of a cliff a hundred metres high. Covering over four hectares in area, it is defended by three semi-circular terraced walls of dry masonry. Between the middle and outer walls hundreds of jagged limestone pillars are wedged into the rocky ground. This pattern of *chevaux-de-frise* must have had a defensive purpose. There is a narrow diagonal passage through it, and the terraces on the inner wall provide a splendid view of the island itself, of the Atlantic Ocean, and of the Galway coast.

Dún Aonghusa was probably constructed in the final centuries BC, and scholars have put forward many and varying theories as to its builders and their purpose. Some regard it as possible evidence for an early settlement in Ireland by peoples from Spain, but the more generally held view is that it represents an expansion westwards of Celtic building methods from Belgium through Britain into Ireland. Mediaeval Irish literature seems to support this, when it claims that the fortress belonged to the Fir Bolg, a semi-mythical group of ancient Celtic settlers in Ireland, one of whose leaders bore the name Aonghus. It has also been suggested that religious ritual was more important at the site than military defence, though the elaborate defences would argue against this. The general situation would suggest that it originally belonged to a group of people who had retreated from the mainland to the Aran Islands, and who felt themselves beleaguered there.

Church of Mac Dara
County Galway

This church was built after the fashion of timber-construction but with large granite stones, and with a stone roof, on the island of Cruach Mhac Dara, west of Carna in Conamara. It is a small building, under five metres in length and just over three metres in breadth. Nearby stands a square stone altar, three 'stations' with crosses, and a holy well. All of these remains, as well as the island itself, are dedicated to St. Sionnach Mac Dara. A wooden statue of the saint was preserved in the church down through the ages, until the Archbishop of Tuam had it removed in the 17th century. Strong devotion to this saint survives locally, and his 'pattern' (celebration of his festival) takes place annually on the island on July 16.

Little is known for certain concerning Mac Dara, but he seems to have lived in the 6th century. Folk belief and legend is expansive concerning him. It was customary for boats, when passing by the island, to lower their sails three times in honour of the saint, and the belief was that this protected them from rough seas on their voyage. A story is told that Mac Dara, when he first came to the island, brought some cattle and sheep with him. Raiders soon took away his ram and his bull, however, leaving him without any prospect of replenishing his stock. As he was dejectedly considering this situation, a new ram and bull swam across from the mainland to him, and the marks of their hooves where they landed on the island are still pointed out.

Croagh Patrick
County Mayo

The mission of St. Patrick to Ireland took place in the 5th century, and legends concerning him developed quickly. According to a biography written in the 7th century he once retired to the great mountain in the west called Cruachán Aighle. We read that he spent forty days and forty nights praying on top of that mountain, and was somewhat discomfited by the great number of birds there. Another biography, some generations later, claims that this was Patrick's observance of Lent, and that the birds there were the demons of paganism trying to distract him. He banished them by ringing his bell, after which angelic birds came and sang melodiously for him. Patrick refused to leave the mountain or abandon his fast until God consented to give him the right to judge all the Irish people on the Last Day.

In memory of this famous episode, the mountain has long been known simply as Cruach Phádraig ('Patrick's Rick'). It is indeed possible that the saint was well acquainted with it, as scholars consider that most of his period as a boy slave was spent in its vicinity. The towering mountain rises to a height of 765 metres over Clew Bay, and thousands of people climb to the summit each year on the last Sunday in July. Prayers are said and Mass is celebrated on the summit, from which there is a magnificent view of the scores of islands in the bay beneath. This penitential pilgrimage to Croagh Patrick has existed for centuries, and some people still do the climb in their bare feet.

Turoe Stone
County Galway

This great granite stone, over a metre in height and weighing several tonnes, stands at Turoe, near Bullaun about six kilometres north of Loughrea. It was moved to this location in the 1850s, having formerly stood on the nearby low hill, on the summit of which was *Ráth an Fhir Mhóir* ('the rath of the Big Man'). In its original form, the stone was deposited at this place by glacial drift in the Ice Age, but in the 1st century BC or thereabouts a skilled mason hammered and chiselled it into its present shape. He then smoothed and ornamented it with a pattern of quadrangles around its middle and abstract curvilinear designs stretching right around its upper part and meeting at the top.

The designs are similar to ones found on several other objects in Ireland, being of a type which was spread by the Celts across western Europe from the 5th century BC onwards. This is known as the La Tène style, and its occurrence in the west of Ireland at such an early period suggests that Celtic culture was already well established in the country. It is an impressive monument to social changes in an obscure historical period, and plays a major role in a more general scholarly debate as to whether Celtic culture was spread by conquest or by acculturation. Almost as difficult to decide is the actual purpose fulfilled by the Turoe stone. It may have been simply a territorial marker, but the fact that it stood near to a rath dating from the same period and that it has a phallic shape would suggest that its function was ritual.

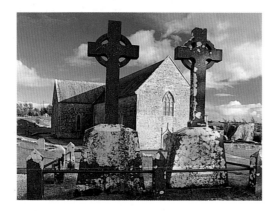

Ballintober Abbey
County Mayo

There was an ancient monastery at *Baile an Tobair* ('the townland of the well'), to the immediate north of Lough Carra. Here, in 1216, the shrewd and able King of Connacht, Cathal 'Crobhdhearg' Ó Conchúir, half-brother to the last High-King of Ireland, founded an Augustinian Abbey. It consists of a cruciform church with nave, transepts, and choir. The general design shows a combination of Late Romanesque and Early Gothic styles, such as in the fine doorway, surrounded by a lofty gable, the pointed windows in the nave, and the round-headed windows in the east end. The church was repaired after fire-damage in 1265, and cloisters were added in the 15th century. The abbey was unroofed and otherwise damaged by Cromwell's soldiers in 1653, but it continued to be used for Mass and was partially restored in the 18th century and more fully in recent times.

Its founder, King Cathal, was long remembered as a great patron of the monks. It was said that he built the abbey in appreciation of the protection that they gave him and his mother when he was threatened in his youth by rival relatives. He got his nickname *Crobhdhearg* ('red-hand') from a birthmark on his right hand, which was taken to foretell his future greatness. Folklore claims that he went about for a long time as a fugitive in disguise, covering his red hand with a glove. He was working as a migrant labourer in Leinster when the kingship of the province became vacant. He returned home, proved his identity by removing the glove, and announced, 'Goodbye to the sickle, now for the sword!'

Benbulben Mountain

County Sligo

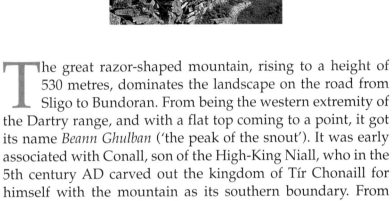

The great razor-shaped mountain, rising to a height of 530 metres, dominates the landscape on the road from Sligo to Bundoran. From being the western extremity of the Dartry range, and with a flat top coming to a point, it got its name *Beann Ghulban* ('the peak of the snout'). It was early associated with Conall, son of the High-King Niall, who in the 5th century AD carved out the kingdom of Tír Chonaill for himself with the mountain as its southern boundary. From this circumstance, the adventurous young man became known as Conall Gulban.

According to an old legend, Conall was fostered in the area by a druid, who was determined to build up the strength of his young protegé. With this in mind, the druid set him to running each day from a pillar-stone at the base as far up the steep mountainside as he could. The youth managed to run further each day, until eventually he reached the top without pausing. Benbulben is also featured in the story of the elopement of the handsome Diarmaid with Gráinne, a maiden who had been betrothed to the aging Fionn Mac Cumhaill. After chasing the young lovers through the length and breadth of Ireland, Fionn pretended to accept a reconciliation, but tricked Diarmaid into hunting the savage boar of Benbulben. Fionn knew that it was destined for this boar and Diarmaid to die together, and in a ferocious contest both man and beast expired. The poet W. B. Yeats, who was enthralled by the lore associated with the mountain, willed that he should be buried 'under bare Benbulben's head in Drumcliff churchyard'.

LEINSTER

Kilkenny Castle

Newgrange Passage-Tomb
County Meath

This great burial mound was constructed nearly 5,000 years ago. Overlooking the river Boyne, it is about 100 metres in diameter and almost 15 metres in height, and would have required hundreds of workers to pile up its 200,000 tonnes of material. The powerful Stone Age people, whose cult-centre it was, dominated the whole northern midlands of Ireland, but we have no clue as to the language they spoke and can only speculate on their customs and beliefs. Not only were they great builders, but they also specialised in abstract art, as is clear from the many spirals, lozenges, triangles, zig-zags, and cup-marks inscribed on the kerbstones which girdle the mound.

A long passage-way leads to the centre of the mound, which is in cruciform shape, with three recesses and a granite basin in each. Cremated bones in these recesses suggest that the basins contained the remains of chieftains. Most remarkably, a 'roof-box' is located over the entrance, and at the winter solstice the sun shines directly through this and lights up the whole passage. The nurturing sun took away the spirits of the dead chieftains and guaranteed the welfare of the people under their new leaders. When the Celts reached Ireland in the final centuries BC, they echoed this ritual and regarded the place as the residence of their own great father-deity, the sun-like Daghdha. They called it *Brugh na Bóinne* ('the hostel of the Boyne'), and – probably echoing the earlier tradition – told a story of how the Daghdha handed over the place to his son Aenghus, a divinely handsome youth.

Jerpoint Abbey
County Kilkenny

This is the magnificent ruin of a Cistercian abbey founded around the year 1160 by the king of Ossory, Donncha Mac Giolla Phádraig. It was under the patronage of the Virgin Mary, and its first abbot was Felix Ó Dubhshláine, later to become Bishop of Ossory and whose effigy can be seen carved on a tomb in the chancel. The church is about 50 metres long and 25 metres in width, and consists of chancels, transept chapels, and nave with side aisles. In the 15th century the lofty square tower was erected, being raised on four arches – three of these are in Gothic style, and the fourth is rounded.

The Norman conquest came within a dozen years of the foundation of Jerpoint, and the abbey soon found itself under pressure to conform with the new control of ecclesiastical affairs. Contrary to Norman policy, Jerpoint continued to admit native Irishmen as monks, and as a result its influence over sister-houses was reduced. Its future was, however, guaranteed by the protection of strong Norman families of the locality. The more elaborate stone carvings in the abbey date from the 15th and 16th centuries and are the work of a special school of masons located some miles away at Callan. These worked under the patronage of the Butlers, Lords of Ormond, but they were inspired by the art-forms found in the illuminated manuscripts of early Irish Christianity. The most celebrated of them was Ruairí Ó Tuine, who carved the effigy of a harper and his wife that is in a room next to the chapter house.

Townhouses

Dublin City

The 18th century, under the reign of the Georges, ushered in a period of great housebuilding in Dublin. Many of the fine houses were town dwellings for the new gentry who had received vast estates in rural Ireland due to their loyalty to the Hanoverian dynasty. St. Stephen's Green was laid out to provide sites for such houses, and this was followed soon afterwards by the formation of Dawson Street, Grafton Street, and Molesworth Street, after which the building extended to Merrion Square, Fitwilliam Square, and areas north of the river Liffey. The beauty of the houses in all that area remains as a testimony to an age of affluence among the ruling class, and to their fine taste in design and architecture.

These townhouses have a basement, topped by four storeys, and are built in terraces with long brick façades. They have impressive doorways, the lintel resting on two pillars and an arched fanlight overhead. The vertical rectangular windows are in two shafts and are multi-paned, while internally the ceilings were often decorated in Neo-Classical style. As the century wore on, successful merchants and businessmen became more numerous as neighbours of the gentry, but the latter continued to attract most of the attention with their more colourful lifestyles. One of the houses on St. Stephen's Green, for instance, was the residence of the celebrated rake and daredevil, Thomas 'Buck' Whaley. It was said that – for a bet – Whaley once rode his horse in a flying jump through an open window of the house, over a stagecoach in the street outside, and landed safely on a hay-cart.

Anna Livia Sculpture

Dublin City

The ancient Celts believed that rivers, on which agricultural success depended and around which settlements usually formed, had divine protection. It was usual in Ireland, as in other Celtic areas, to dedicate each river to a particular goddess. Thus, whereas some rivers had descriptive names, others were so closely identified with a goddess as to actually bear her name. The river on which the city of Dublin stands was anciently known as the *Ruirtheach* (meaning 'the rapid flowing one'). It has a semi-circular configuration, flowing westwards from the Wicklow mountains into the plain of Kildare and then turning eastwards again to enter the sea at Dublin.

The ancient name for the basin of this river was 'the plain of Liphe'. The identity of Liphe (later written *Life*) is unknown, but a mediaeval poem claims that she was the noble wife of a warrior and that she died in childbirth. At any rate, due to its flowing through this area, the *Ruirtheach* was often referred to as the river of this plain, *Abha na Life*. In anglicised form this was rendered as Anna Livia, which the writer James Joyce used as a suitable pun to resurrect the old tradition of river-goddesses. Thus a modern myth was created of the river Liffey as a lady symbolising Dublin. This was dramatised in the sculpture by Eamonn O'Doherty, which since 1988 has adorned O'Connell Street in the city centre. Anna Livia in bronze reclines in water, surrounded by Wicklow granite. The wags of Dublin have given a humorous twist to the myth by nicknaming the work 'the Floozy in the Jacuzzi'!

Statue of Daniel O'Connell

Dublin City

One of the most celebrated of all Irish political leaders, Daniel O'Connell (1775-1847) was known as 'the Liberator'. He excelled as a defence lawyer in the oppressive courts system of his time, saving scores of people from the gallows by his brilliant and incisive knowledge of law. Elected for County Clare as a Member of Parliament, he soon showed his skills at Westminster also, gaining Catholic Emancipation in 1829. In the following decade, he led a massive popular campaign to secure an independent parliament for Ireland but, confronted by the threat of British force, he backed down to avoid bloodshed and died a broken man in Italy as the Great Famine raged in his native country.

A native of County Kerry, O'Connell was elected Lord Mayor of Dublin in 1841 at the height of his political power and, some time after his death, it was decided to commemorate him with a great statue in that city. The figure of O'Connell addressing a mass meeting is by John Henry Foley, who died in 1874 before the full monument was completed. Thomas Brock then added the lady Ireland casting off her fetters, and the winged figures representing patriotism, fidelity, eloquence, and courage. The monument stands in the main thoroughfare of the city, later renamed 'O'Connell Street'. The memory of 'Immortal Dan' is evergreen in Irish folklore. A well-known story tells of him being invited to a great feast in London, at which an Irish servant-girl was serving the food. She spoke a verse to Daniel in Irish warning him that his drink was poisoned, whereupon he quietly exchanged his glass with that of the treacherous host.

Statue of Cú Chulainn
Dublin City

Cú Chulainn was the most dramatic hero in Irish epic. Originating in the warrior-cult of an Iron Age people in the area of County Louth, he was adopted into the tales of the Ulster heroes by storytellers from the 8th century onwards and was made the dominant figure in the great literary tale of *Táin Bó Cuailgne* ('the Cattle Raid of Cooley'). In this, he defends the province of Ulster single-handedly against the mighty army of Queen Meadhbh of Connacht, who is trying to take away by force a great brown bull. Other accounts of Cú Chulainn were soon added – such as how he killed a mighty hound while yet a boy, how his body became monstrously distorted in battle, and how he tamed two mighty stallions to draw his chariot. Prohibited by honour from refusing an invitation to a feast, and by his name (*cú* = 'hound') from eating dog-meat, he was trapped when his enemies offered him such a feast. He ate the meat, but his strength left him, and he was treacherously slain.

Cú Chulainn has long been regarded as a champion of the Gaelic people of both Ireland and Scotland. He was a major persona in the poetry and drama of W. B. Yeats, and was taken by Pádraic Pearse as a character symbolising Irish revolutionary vigour. The 1916 Rising against British rule, led by Pearse in the General Post Office in Dublin, saw the acting out in modern times of the spirit of Cú Chulainn, who willingly chose death rather than shame. The statue in bronze, by Oliver Sheppard, stands in the General Post Office in recognition of that ideal.

Trinity College
Dublin City

In the 12th century, the Leinster king Diarmaid Mac Murchadha established the Augustinian Priory of All Hallows in Dublin at the site of an old well dedicated to St. Patrick. The ruins of the priory were long dilapidated when, in 1591, by charter of Queen Elizabeth I, 'the College of the Holy and Undivided Trinity' was established. The purpose of the new College was to prevent young Irishmen going abroad for education and being infected by anti-English feeling in France, Italy, and Spain, and its first Provost was Adam Loftus. Initially open to all religions, Trinity College became increasingly a bastion of the Protestant ascendancy, but from the 18th century onwards it gradually abandoned its exclusive character.

Little of the original structure of this celebrated academic establishment survives, as the buildings were reconstructed in the 18th century and extended repeatedly since then. As it stands, the whole site is a treasure-house of architecture, art-work, monuments, statues, and other artefacts. Innumerable scholars, politicians, and clergymen have passed through its doors. Some of the most famous of these were the writers William Congreve, Jonathan Swift, Oliver Goldsmith, Oscar Wilde, John Millington Synge, and Samuel Beckett; the philosopher George Berkeley; the mathematician William Rowan Hamilton and the scientist Ernest Walton. Former students who played leading roles in Irish history included the politicians Henry Grattan, Edmund Burke, John Fitzgibbon, and Edward Carson; and the patriots Theobald Wolfe Tone, Robert Emmet, Thomas Davis, and John Mitchel. The massive Library, established as early as 1602, by Luke Challoner and James Ussher, is one of the finest in Europe and contains many invaluable manuscripts.

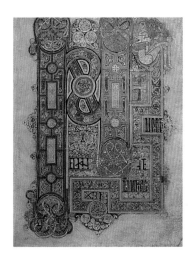

The Book of Kells

Trinity College, Dublin City

In the year 563 AD St. Columba left Ireland and founded a monastery on the small island of Iona, west of Mull in Scotland. This became a great centre of missionary activity and of learning, but Viking raids forced most of the monks to abandon it in the year 806. They settled at *Ceanannas* (Kells) in County Meath, where the building of a fine new monastery was completed eight years later. The transfer of the monastic community coincided with the writing of a great manuscript on vellum, which apparently was begun at Iona and finished at Kells, and it is from the name of the new location that the work is now known.

The Book of Kells is one of the finest illuminated manuscripts in the world. It contains the Four Gospels along with some notational material, all in Latin. Its semi-uncial script is lavishly decorated, with over two thousand ornamented capital letters. There is a profusion of representations of people, angels, animals, and abstract figures, while several full pages are devoted to illustrations of Christ and of the Evangelists. The detail and intricacy of the art-work is astounding, and bears witness to the devotion and skill of the scribes. In the year 1007, this invaluable manuscript was stolen, and its golden cover ripped off. It was recovered within three months, lying under a sod with some pages torn away, and the surviving 340 leaves were brought back to Kells. After the closure of the monastery in 1539, the Book was kept in Dublin and was acquired by Trinity College in 1661.

Kilkenny Castle

County Kilkenny

In the year 1192, one of the leading Norman conquerors, William Marshal, built a large castle on an eminence over the river Nore. Soon after, King John granted control of the wine patent for the whole of Ireland to Theobald, brother of the Archbishop of Canterbury. From this Theobald derived his surname *de Bouteillier* ('bottle-bearer'); but the later Butlers turned it into a myth whereby their great ancestor had landed in Arklow, unsheathed his sword there and formally announced that he would not rest until he had control of the whole island. He did not achieve that, but his descendants intermarried with those of Marshal, and in 1391 the great castle of Kilkenny was acquired by James Butler, 3rd Earl of Ormond.

From that time on, Kilkenny Castle has been synonymous with the Butler family. The occupants have been varied and dramatic, including the 8th Earl Piaras Rua Butler (+1539) and his wife Margaret, famed for her appetite; their grandson Black Tom (1532-1614), who was reputed to have enchanted pistols that guaranteed victory in any duel; the Machiavellian James, created 1st Duke of Ormond (1607-1688), who was the leading Irish political figure of his day. This James remodelled the castle and immense grounds on French patterns in the 17th century, by removing the defences, erecting the Classical entrance, and placing lofty roofs on the towers. The whole structure was again remodelled in the 19th century, this time in the castellated style, and the great picture gallery was designed by Benjamin Woodward. The castle was presented by the Marquess of Ormond to the people of Kilkenny in 1967.

St. Canice's Cathedral

County Kilkenny

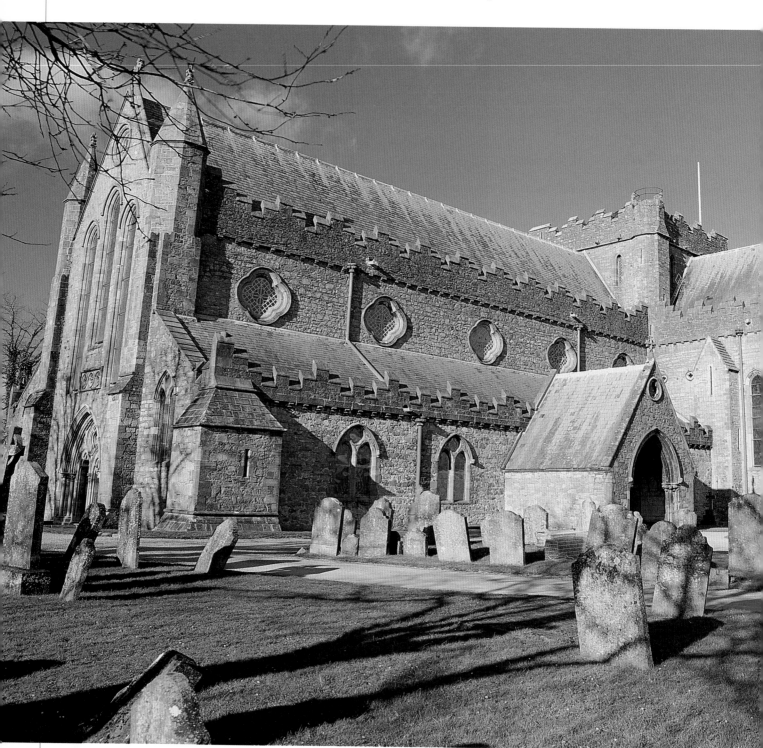

ainneach (anglicised 'Canice'), was born in the vicinity of Derry, and was one of the monks of Columba on the island of Iona, off the Scottish coast. He was celebrated for his scholarship, eloquence, and beautiful writing. Around the year 580 he returned to Ireland and established a monastery at Aghaboe in County Laois. Some time later, he founded a smaller church further south, at a place which came to be known as *Cill Chainnigh* ('the cell of Cainneach', hence Kilkenny). By the 9th century, this latter foundation had grown into a large monastic and commercial centre, and a round tower – over 30 metres high – was constructed. In the year 1111, the see of Ossory was transferred from Aghaboe to Kilkenny, and a cathedral-church was built there.

A new cathedral in Gothic style was constructed on the site in the 13th century. The plan is cruciform, with chapels and other accessory buildings at both sides of the chancel. It is over 68 metres in length, and 39 metres in breadth across the transepts. In 1332, the belfry collapsed and damaged the side chapels, and as part of the repairs beautiful stained glass windows were installed, but these were destroyed when the army of Oliver Cromwell took Kilkenny in 1650. It is said that Cromwell stabled his horses in the cathedral and seated himself atop the belfry in order to view the city. The building contains the tombs of nobility and ecclesiastics from the 14th to the 16th century, with fine effigies; but some of its features are due to the general restoration, which was carried out in 1866.

Powerscourt Demesne

County Wicklow

The lands of the chieftain, Féilim Ó Tuathail, at Teach Chonaill, were taken over by the Elizabethan officer, Sir Richard Wingfield, in the 16th century. Local lore claims that the chieftain was ambushed and slain by Wingfield while riding out alone one morning at a place called 'the Killing Hollow' on the modern estate. The Wingfields became one of the most powerful landlord families in Ireland, and they renamed the place as Powerscourt. In the 1730s another Richard – later the first Viscount Powerscourt – engaged Richard Cassels to construct a magnificent new house for him there. Cassels was a renowned architect, who came to Ireland from Germany in 1727 and who also built Leinster House and the Rotunda Hospital in Dublin, Carton House in County Kildare, and Russborough House in County Wicklow.

The beautiful terraces by Daniel Robertson were laid out between 1843 and 1875, and the Japanese Garden was added in 1908. The demesne is enormous, and offers a magnificent view southwards towards the Sugarloaf mountain. Also in the demesne, though at some distance from the house, is a steep waterfall, where the river Dargle pitches more than a hundred metres over a narrow precipice. It is said that, in the 19th century, a descendant of Féilim Ó Tuathail, when inebriated, used to go to Powerscourt and shout out in colourful language for his place to be given back to him. When arrested and brought to court, he usually got off with a small fine, for the presiding magistrate was Lord Powerscourt! The house was gutted in an accidental fire in 1974.

St. Laurence's Gate

Drogheda, County Louth

There was a monastery since early Christian times at the mouth of the river Boyne, at a place known as Droichead Átha ('the bridge at the ford'). The Vikings seized this area in the year 911 AD, but the monastery survived until the 12th century, when its community was replaced by Norman monks. The Norman lord, Hugh de Lacy, fortified a mound on the southern side of the river and built a new bridge; and in the 13th century walls, over 2,000 metres in circumference, were constructed to enclose the surrounding area on both sides of the river. The new town became known in English as Drogheda. It was one of the chief centres of power in Ireland during the 14th and 15th centuries, and several parliaments were held there.

Drogheda remained loyal to King Charles I during the English Civil War, and it was defended by Sir Arthur Aston against the forces of Oliver Cromwell in 1649. Cromwell took the town by storm, and then ordered a general massacre of its inhabitants. Within a generation, however, the town had recovered and had resumed its flourishing corn-trade. Originally, there were four gates in the walls of Drogheda, each protected by two towers. None of the gates survives, but the two towers which guarded St. Laurence's Gate – so called from the priory of St. Laurence that once stood nearby – are still in situ. The towers are circular, each 6 metres in circumference and over 15 metres high. They have battlements on top, and are linked together by a curtain of stone. In medieval times, a moat was between this barbican structure and the actual town wall.

The Cross of Muireadhach

Monasterboice, County Louth

Little is known for definite concerning St. Buithe, except that he belonged to the early 6th century. His parents were probably already Christians, as his name seems to be an Irish adaptation of the Latin Boethius. Although later fanciful accounts claim that he spent some time in Scotland on a mission to the Picts, it is unlikely that he ever travelled far from his native territory, where he founded the small monastery that took its name from him, *Mainistir Bhuithe* (anglicised as Monasterboice). The foundation gradually grew in importance, and by the 10th century two churches, a round tower, and three high crosses adorned the site. In the 11th century, the monastery's Latin master was Flann, a Gaelic poet who wrote valuable descriptions of the pre-Christian mythology of Ireland.

The high-cross erected by Muireadhach, abbot of Monasterboice from 899 to 924, is the finest of its type in Ireland, being totally covered in ornamentation. It is almost five and a half metres in height, and the tradition – probably unreliable – is that it was cut from a single stone which had been sent by the Pope to Ireland. The base has a variety of animal figures, and each of the two sides gives instruction on major Christian doctrines. The east face presents sacred history – Adam and Eve, Abel, David, Moses, the Epiphany, the Church's Mission, and the General Judgement. On the west face the motifs all have to do with the Salvation of Man by Christ's Passion, Crucifixion, Resurrection, Ascension, and Founding of the Church. The summit of the cross is in the shape of a shingle-roofed church with gables.

Clonmacnoise
County Offaly

St. Ciarán was said to have been the son of an Antrim father and a Kerry mother, and to have shown his great holiness from an early age. Early accounts describe him as a very charitable and sympathetic man, who ransomed captives and befriended the poor. He struck up a strong friendship with the half-Christian half-pagan king of Tara, Diarmaid mac Ceirrbheoil, who in 545 AD assisted him in founding the celebrated monastery of *Cluain Mhac Nóis* (Clonmacnoise). Ciarán lived for only nine months as abbot, but his foundation grew into the greatest educational centre in Ireland and claimed wide ecclesiastical jurisdiction.

Situated in beautiful surroundings, and overlooking the wide expanse of the river Shannon, Clonmacnoise has eight churches, two round towers, two holy wells, and hundreds of memorial slabs. It also has three high crosses, of which the elaborately illustrated Cross of the Scriptures is the main attraction. In the year 844, the pagan Viking warlord Thorgest burned Clonmacnoise, and his wife sat on the principal altar delivering oracles. In succeeding centuries, the monastery survived many other attacks by Viking, native Irish, and English raiders, and it played a leading role in the development of literature in the Irish language. Among the manuscripts produced there was the great 11th-century compilation *Lebor na hUidre* ('the book of the dun cow'). Later lore claimed that this manuscript was written on the skin of a cow which had followed Ciarán to Clonmacnoise and given a copious milk supply to all the monks there. The site was once more pillaged and left in complete ruins by the English garrison from Athlone in 1552.

Christchurch Cathedral

Dublin City

When the raiding Norsemen sailed up the mouth of the Liffey in 837 AD, there was a pre-existing small Irish settlement on the northern bank, where the Four Courts now stand. This settlement was called *Baile Átha Cliath* ('the town of the wattle ford'), from a crossing of the river there. Within fifteen years the newcomers had founded their own settlement on the opposite bank, a few hundred metres nearer to the bay, at a place where the river was then wider, and was thus called by the Irish *Dubh-linn* ('black pool'). This new fortified town grew into the strong Norse kingdom of Dublin.

These Norsemen in time became Christianised, and the original Christchurch was founded by their king Sigtrygg Silkbeard in or about 1038 AD, but their power was overthrown when the Normans captured Dublin in 1171. The Norman leader Richard de Clare ('Strongbow') determined to replace the church with a new cathedral, and the building of this began almost immediately. Strongbow himself was buried there on his death in 1176, and the work was completed by 1234, with an Augustinian priory on the southern side. The priory was dissolved in 1539, and the Roman liturgy was replaced by the Anglican in 1551. The building was badly dilapidated before it was restored, in Gothic style and with drastic alterations, in the 1870s by George Edmund Street. He rebuilt the tower, and added the present Chapter House. He also incorporated the old bell-tower into a new Synod Hall, linking it to the cathedral by the covered footbridge which spans the adjacent roadway.

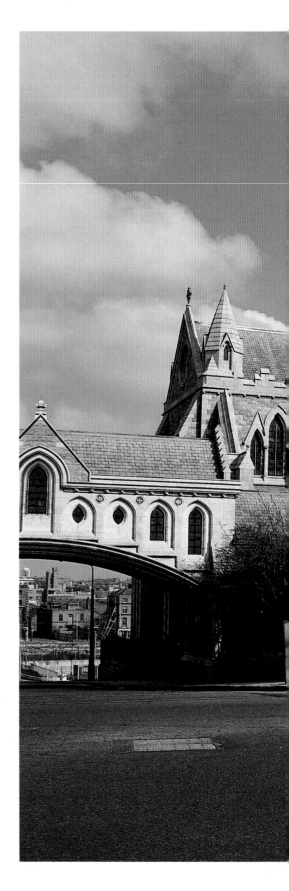

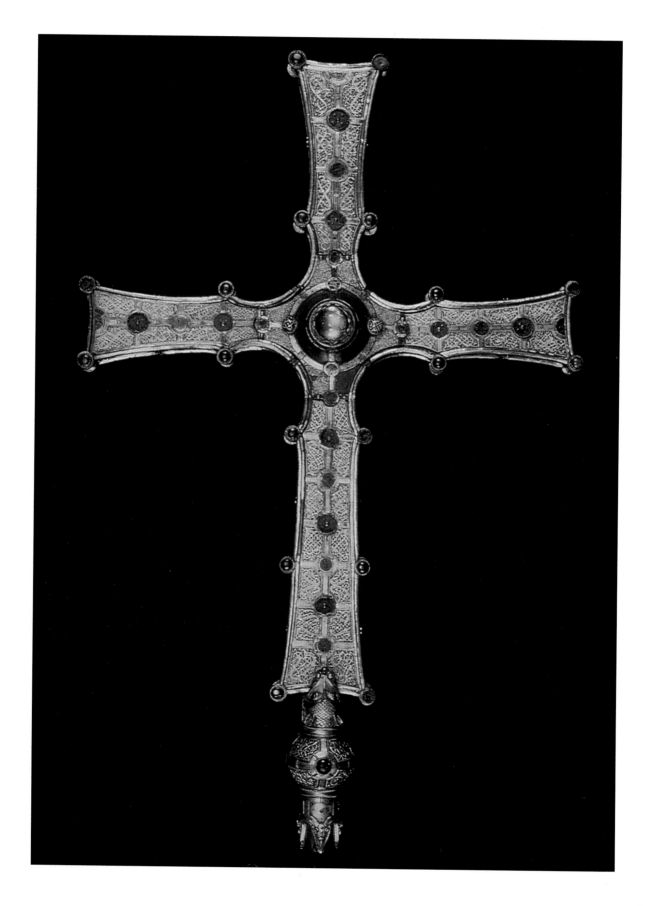

The Cross of Cong

National Museum of Ireland, Dublin City

After a period of uncertainty, the king of Connacht, Toirdhealbhach Mór Ó Conchúir, emerged in 1119 as the leading figure among competing dynasties and established himself as High-King of Ireland. From his strong headquarters in the west, he impressed his rule on the other provinces and became a great patron of learning and of the Church. The most striking artefact to survive from his reign is a Cross for use in processions, the work of Maol Íosa Ó hEacháin at Roscommon in or about the year 1123. Known as the *Bachall Bhuí* ('yellow staff'), the Cross is 76 by 48 centimetres in size, and was made by order of Toirdhealbhach to enshrine a supposed piece of the True Cross. It consists of bronze plates on an oak foundation, beautifully decorated with studs of red and green glass and with interlacing animal-designs in gold. The relic was covered at the centre of the Cross by a large rock crystal.

Among Toirdhealbhach's other acts of patronage of the Church was the foundation in 1128 of an Augustinian abbey at a place called *Cunga* ('neck' – it being the isthmus between Lough Corrib and Lough Mask). Toirdhealbhach died in 1152 and was succeeded by his son Ruairí, the last High-King of Ireland. After the Norman conquest, Ruairí retired to Cong Abbey in 1183 and spent the final years of his life in seclusion there. He apparently brought the Cross with him, and it was held in veneration in that vicinity down through the centuries, until presented to the National Museum in 1839.

The Ardagh Chalice

National Museum of Ireland, Dublin City

Local legend has it that an old church at the village of *Ard-Achadh* ('high field', anglicised Ardagh), in County Limerick, was founded by St. Patrick. It is said that the saint was quite hot-tempered, and that he once pronounced a curse on the local people to the effect that a dead body would be found in the place every morning. He soon relented, and said that the curse would apply only to the birds, and thus a dead starling is found there each day.

Less fantastic but even more wonderful was the discovery made by a youth who was digging potatoes at a large ring-fort, just west of the village, in 1868. This youth found, underneath a thorn-bush, four ring-brooches, a small bronze cup, and a chalice which is regarded as one of the finest pieces of metalwork in the world. The Ardagh Chalice dates to the 8th century, the product of a brilliant but anonymous craftsman who was acquainted with Byzantine style but who was working wholly within the Irish tradition. Almost 18 centimetres high and 24 centimetres in diameter, it is perfectly proportioned and wrought from silver, gold, and bronze, with rich settings of crystal, glass, amber, and enamel. It is estimated that hundreds of separate parts went into the making of the Chalice, each part bearing testimony to the brilliance and skill of the craftsman. It must have belonged to one of the larger monasteries in Munster, and is thought to have been buried in order to save it from the hands of Viking plunderers in or about the 10th century.

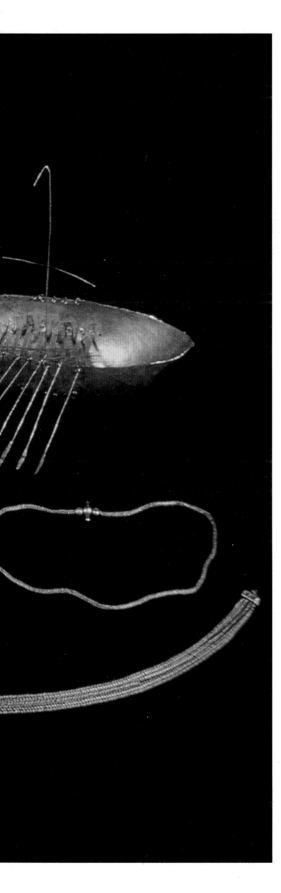

The Broighter Hoard

National Museum of Ireland, Dublin City

In the year 1896, two ploughmen were working in the townland of Broighter, on the shore of Lough Foyle a few kilometres west of Limavady in County Derry. To their great surprise, they turned up a small hoard of golden objects, which they sold to their employer for five pounds sterling. After a stirring controversy concerning the proper institution in which it should be kept, the hoard ended up in the National Museum in Dublin. It dates to the 1st century BC, and consists of a torque or neck-ring, a bowl with loops attached, four wire necklaces, some pins, and a beautiful little model boat. All are in the general style of Celtic Europe.

The torque – over 19 centimetres in diameter and about 3 centimetres wide – is broken in the centre and lacks the design on one of its heads. Its ornamentation is superb, consisting of curvilinear motifs in high relief, and most of the designs must have been executed on the two flat sheets of gold with which the artist began. These sheets were then rolled into cylinders, which were filled with sand so that they could be twisted into half-circles before being joined. The boat – nearly 20 centimetres long – is fitted out with fifteen oars, nine seats and a mast with a yard-arm for a sail. The fact that it was discovered at Broighter (*Brú Íochtair*, 'the lower bank'), near to the coast, suggests that the hoard might well have been a votive deposit. In that case, the little boat would have been a ritual replica to invoke protection at sea.

Glendalough
County Wicklow

The name of this place, *Gleann Dá Loch*, means 'the valley of two lakes', and it is one of the most scenic parts of Ireland. The Upper Lake is an extraordinarily deep declivity between two mountains; whereas the Lower Lake, 600 metres to the north, is in more open surroundings and is smaller and more shallow. The valley is home to buildings and structures ranging from the Bronze Age right up to the mediaeval period. Earliest are a circular stone fort, a hill-side cave, an early Christian hermit-cell, several small churches, and a cemetery with a fine cross, while the larger churches, the cathedral, and the round tower, are of somewhat later date. It was claimed that a pilgrimage done to Glendalough was the equivalent of one to Rome, and hundreds of students resorted to the monastery for both ecclesiastical and secular studies.

The valley is most intimately associated with the celebrated St. Kevin (*Caoimhghin*), founder of the original monastic settlement around the year 600 AD. Many legends are told of him, in which he is described as an austere but kindly man, a great friend of the poor and of birds and animals. He is said to have performed severe Lenten penance, including standing in the water up to his waist for long periods and fasting continuously while lying on a cold slab. One story has it that, on Kevin's first arrival in the valley, he banished a huge reptilian monster from the Lower Lake. The monster still abides in the depths of the Upper Lake, and when it turns on its side the water rises as high as the surrounding mountains!

Michael Dwyer Cottage
Derrynamuck, County Wicklow

The Rising of 1798 was one of the most momentous and significant events of Irish history, the revolutionary movement of the time combining ancient grievances with the international demand for the rights of man, and striving to unite Irish people of different cultural backgrounds and different religious persuasions. The actual rebellion was precipitated by savage government measures, and most of the fighting was done in three regions – east Ulster, west Connacht, and particularly in Wexford and adjacent parts of south Leinster. After a few months of fighting, the insurgent forces were crushed and tens of thousands slain, participants and non-participants alike.

In one area only did resistance continue, and that for five years under the guerrilla leader Michael Dwyer in the mountain fastnesses of Wicklow. Dwyer was daring and resourceful, inflicting many casualties on the Redcoat soldiers, and massive efforts to capture him ended in failure. He eventually managed to negotiate conditions for his departure to Australia. One of his narrowest escapes took place on the night of February 15, 1799, when a farmer's cottage in Derrynamuck in south-west Wicklow was surrounded by a large troop of soldiers. Sleeping inside were Dwyer and three companions. In the furious exchange of fire, two of them were killed, and the third was seriously wounded. This was Sam McAllister, a rebel who had come south from Antrim and was Dwyer's closest confidant. In a generous act of self-sacrifice, McAllister appeared in the doorway, deliberately drawing the fire of the soldiers and enabling Dwyer to rush out barefoot behind him and to make his getaway through a hail of bullets.

Kilmainham Historical Prison

Dublin City

This place takes its name *Cill Mhaighneann* from St. Maighniu who founded his church there in the late 6th century. Maighniu was celebrated as a wise counsellor and prophet, and as a kindly man whose motto was 'What you consider a bad deed to be done to yourself, never do that to anybody else!' His church grew into a monastery, which gave rise to the village of Old Kilmainham. Of the monastery only a small graveyard with the shaft of a high cross now remains. After the Norman invasion, a fortified priory of the Knights Hospitallers was established nearby.

The English rulers built a County Jail on the site of the old monastery in the 17th century, and in 1796 this was replaced by a larger prison on Kilmainham Commons, a little to the west. Thus the earlier atmosphere of gentle sainthood had given way to a harsh régime of incarceration. There was plenty of demand for prison spaces, especially after the crushing of the 1798 Rebellion, and until it closed in 1924 Kilmainham Prison included among its inmates some of the most famous personalities in Irish history. Henry Joy MacCracken was held there, as were Thomas Russell, Robert Emmet, Wlliam Smith O'Brien, and John O'Leary. The great parliamentary leader Charles Stewart Parnell was an unwilling guest there for a while in 1881 until released by Prime Minister Gladstone, and in 1883 the group known as the Invincibles were hanged there for the assassination of Lord Cavendish and his secretary in Phoenix Park. The leaders of the 1916 Rising, including Pádraic Pearse and James Connolly, were executed by firing squad at Kilmainham, the place of execution now marked by a simple cross.

Hill of Tara
County Meath

This hill was regarded as a sacred place since neolithic times, no doubt because of the wide view which it provides of the centre of Ireland. From this also it gets its name *Teamhair*, meaning 'spectacle'. The Celts made it a ritual centre of kingship, and in time the rulers of Tara claimed to be High-Kings of all Ireland. The cult of the sun-deity, patron of rulers, was strong there, and the career of the king of Tara was hedged about by several sacred prohibitions. According to the old literature, the king must not sleep on after sunrise there and he must not be abroad after sunset, and he must not travel withershins around the area.

It was said that, when a king of Tara was to be selected, a druid slept on the hide of a white bull, and in his sleep had a vision of the proper candidate for the position. The candidate then drove a chariot drawn by two unbroken stallions, and if he were to be the true king a special stone called out when touched by the axle of the chariot. This was the *Lia Fáil*, a stone of phallic shape which still stands on the hill, and was clearly a symbol of the sun-imbued fertility of kingship. The various monuments at Tara are the remains of thousands of years of activity, but tradition attributes their construction exclusively to a legendary Iron Age king called Cormac Mac Airt. Although no longer inhabited after the 6th century, Tara has remained the symbol of kingship and the locus of epical stories throughout Irish history.

'Brian Boru' Harp

National Museum of Ireland, Dublin City

The harp (*cláirseach*) was for long the principal musical instrument in Ireland. It was rested on the left shoulder while being played, and had metal strings, which were plucked with long finger-nails. The earliest full illustration of the mediaeval Irish harp is engraved in bronze on a little reliquary dating to the 11th or 12th century. The shape was roughly triangular, with the back and pillar curved slightly forward. The best surviving example is a richly decorated harp with a willow sound-board, oak back, and twenty-nine brass strings (originally there were thirty). It is believed to date to the 15th century, but has been repaired in the meantime.

Such harps were common throughout the Gaelic world, and this particular one may have been crafted in Scotland rather than in Ireland. It seems to have belonged to a branch of the great O'Neill family of Ulster, but later tradition associates it with the O'Briens. This is due to a well-known 13th-century poem, which describes a trip to Scotland in order to recover a harp belonging to the latter family. The claim was even made that it had once been the harp of the ancestor of the O'Briens, the famous High-King Brian Boru who defeated the Norsemen in the Battle of Clontarf in 1014. The fanciful identification was made easier by the fact that the arts had flourished under the patronage of Brian. His reign was remembered as a golden age in Ireland, when a beautiful young lady laden with jewellery walked unmolested all the way from Tory Island in the north to Glandore in the south!

The Hill of Allen

County Kildare

The midland region of Ireland from Kildare west almost to the river Shannon was anciently known as Almhu, and at the eastern end of this was 'the hill of Almhu' (*Cnoc Almhan*). This prominent hill rises above the Curragh plain to a height of 206 metres, and its summit gives a remarkable view over a wide area. A small battlemented tower was erected there in 1859.

In ancient times the hill was a cultic site of the Leinstermen, dedicated to the god of light called by the Celtic name Vindos. The name of this deity developed into 'Fionn' in Irish, and he was reputed to have been a great seer and warrior. In the guise of Fionn Mac Cumhaill, he has become the most celebrated personage in all Irish lore. We are told that he had his residence on the hill, and a small mound on the summit was still known until recently as his 'seat' (*Suí Finn*). As a boy, he unwittingly tasted the mystical salmon of the Boyne, which was being cooked for an older seer, and thus he gained his wisdom. He later became leader of the celebrated troop of warriors called the Fianna, and innumerable stories were told of his adventures. Lore of Fionn and his Fianna companions was very popular in Scotland as well as in Ireland. Prose-poems in English concerning these characters by the 18th-century Scottish writer James Macpherson were translated into many languages and were very influential. The Hill of Allen has therefore strong claims to be considered one of the leading sites of cultural heritage in Europe.

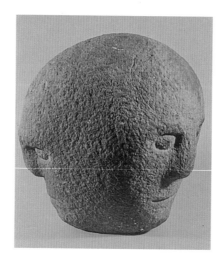

The Corleck Head

National Museum of Ireland, Dublin City

The three-faced head of an idol was a special way in which the Celts expressed the idea of the all-seeing deity. This is a striking example from Ireland, in siliceous sandstone and almost 32 centimetres in height, dating to the 1st century AD or thereabouts. It was found in a quarry on Corleck Hill, a few kilometres north of Bailieborough in County Cavan. The carving is crude and simple, but it conveys an aura of a brooding and rather remote power, which was probably intended by the mason. The three faces share a single massive skull, and there are no ears and no hair. Each visage has a large and powerful brow, circular eyes, rudimentary nose, and a mouth represented by a straight split.

A hole in the bottom of the figure indicates that it was originally placed on top of another stone or a pole, being held in place by a piece of timber. The faces have the clear appearance of an elderly man, and the sculpture can therefore be taken to represent the ancestor god from which all the Celts believed themselves to be descended. There is plenty of evidence that the sun – being the 'eye' of the heavens – was the most usual form in which that deity expressed himself. This gives a special significance to the all-seeing motif of the stone head, for the Celtic druids claimed to partake in the divine propensity of seeing at once into past, present, and future. The stern expressions on the faces, moreover, tend to underline the mystery with which the druids wished to associate themselves.

Sheila-Na-Gig

(various sites)

Scores of such female figures, carved in stone and dating from the 13th to the 17th centuries, have been found on the walls and in the vicinity of churches and castellated dwellings in different parts of Ireland. (Some fine examples are displayed in the National Museum of Ireland, Dublin; those shown here are, left, at Ballyconnell, County Cavan, and, right, at Kilnaboy Church, County Clare.) The figures vary in representation, but they tend to have bulging eyes and gaping mouths, and are all in poses that display their genitalia. It is clear that they were based on somewhat similar carvings on churches, warnings against lust, in other western European countries. These Irish examples concentrate solely on female imagery, however, and it is likely that they came to be interpreted as fertility symbols and that Irish stone-masons treated them as opportunities to demonstrate both their skill and their sense of humour.

In design, the figures seem to owe something to ancient Irish tradition. Effigies of saints and druids which date from several centuries earlier show exaggerated facial features, while some old stories describe mythical heroes as being embarrassed or magically subdued by the appearance of naked women. Like the figures themselves, the term 'Sheila-na-gig' for them has not been satisfactorily explained. It survives only in hiberno-English speech, but appears to be a corruption of an appellation in Irish. This may have been *Síle na Gige* ('Julia of the Scoffing'). Folklore has it that these figures were devices to ward off the power of the evil eye. It was thought that only the first object on which the possessor of such an eye glanced was affected, and the eye would naturally fall on a Sheila-na-gig before taking anything else into account!

The Book of Ó Laoi

Royal Irish Academy, Dublin City

A well-known tradition in the west of County Galway concerns a man called Muircheartach Ó Laoi, whose family were hereditary physicians to the O'Flaherty chieftains. His own profession was not prospering, however, until he suddenly announced that a strange adventure had befallen him. One day in April of the year 1668, he said, he had been accosted on the sea-shore by two strangers, who had forcibly taken him into a boat and blindfolded him. In this way, he had been brought to the otherworld island called *Uí Bhreasail* which lies off the western coast. There, to his surprise, he had been well received, and presented with a marvellous book, before being brought back home again in the same boat. He read the book, which was full of cures and magical remedies, and then began again to practise medicine. Using the knowledge which he had gained, he met with great success and became a famous doctor.

The mysterious book which he used for his cures is still in existence, having been purchased by the Royal Irish Academy in the early 19th century. It is a bound vellum manuscript of 92 pages, some of which are colourfully illustrated, and contains medical data in Latin and Irish of the type common several centuries ago. The claim by Muircheartach has, as one might expect, not been accepted by scholars, for the book was written in the year 1434, long before his time. Unless, of course, it had been preserved in the meantime by the denizens of the otherworld with the express purpose of presenting it to him!

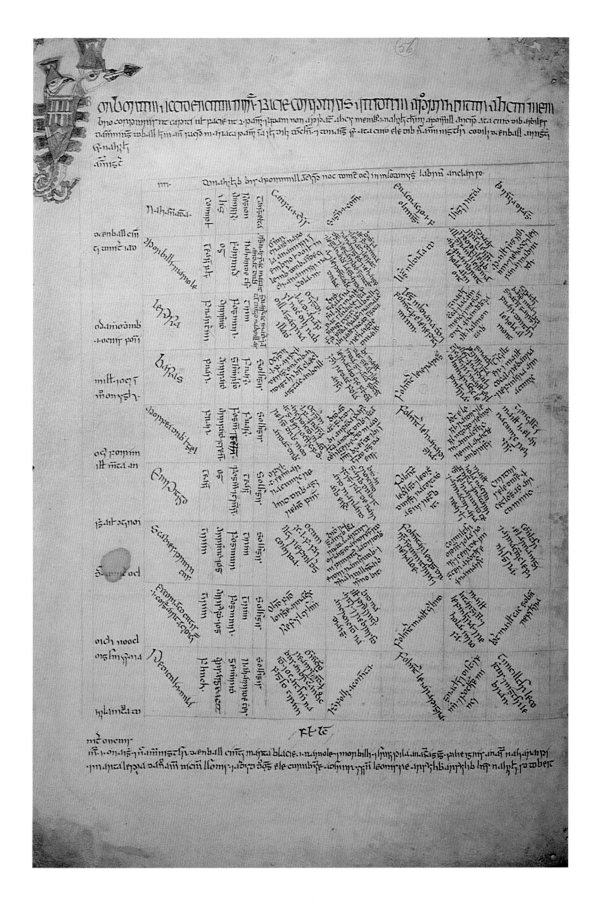

The Cave of Dunmore

County Kilkenny

About nine kilometres to the north of Kilkenny city, at Dunmore, there is a huge natural limestone cavern. Its ancient name was *Deirc Fhearna* ('the hollow among the alders'), and it was said to be 'one of the four dark places of Ireland'. It was considered an entrance to the underworld, and the hero Fionn Mac Cumhaill was anciently said to have fought against sinister beings there. Another mythical story claimed that the cave was the lair of a monster cat called the *Luchthighearn* ('mouse-lord'), which was slain by an Amazonian queen of Leinster called Aithbhéal. This fanciful idea was probably suggested by the shape of the cave-mouth, which resembles the head of a massive cat. Actual history is even more frightening, for it is recorded that, in the year 928, a thousand people were slaughtered here by the Vikings of Dublin under their leader Godfrey.

The cave is over 60 metres in length, and is cold and dank, but its passages and chambers are full of magnificent dripstone formations. The chambers to the left as one enters have many stalactites and a great column. The largest chamber lies to the right, and is popularly known as 'The Fairies' Floor'. Further on one encounters a cluster of oddly shaped blocks, and at the southern extremity lies another chamber, triangular in shape. In the middle of this latter is an enormous stalagmite, called 'The Market Cross' on account of its shape. A footpath of steps has been laid out, with iron railings, as an aid to visitors making the descent into the cave.

Trim Castle
County Meath

In the year 1172 AD, the Viceroy Hugh de Lacy erected a motte with a timber tower at Áth Troim ('the ford of the elder-tree'), on the southern bank of the river Boyne. A Norman captain, Hugh Tyrrell, was left in charge of it. After his death, Lacy's sons, Hugh and Walter, fell foul of King John, who in 1210 took the lordship of Meath from them. Two years later the timber tower was pulled down, and replaced by a massive stone castle. The Lacys were restored to power in 1227, and through marriage with Matilda, grand-daughter of Walter, the castle passed into the possession of Geoffrey de Genville, ancestor of the Mortimers, Earls of the March.

King Richard II visited Trim in 1399, and left as a virtual prisoner there the young Henry of Lancaster, who later became King Henry V. The Viceroy, Richard of York, descendant of the Mortimers and father of King Edward IV, stayed for extended periods there in the later 15th century. The castle was finally abandoned after bombardment by the Cromwellians in 1649. It is the largest Norman fortress in Ireland, the square keep being about 22 metres in height and having walls well over 3 metres thick. Four smaller towers (of which three remain) projected from each of its four faces. The surrounding curtain wall enclosed a total area of over a hectare, but only the southern side remains intact. There are five semi-circular towers in this surviving side, as well as a large rounded tower. Connected to the latter is a barbican, which once spanned the castle's moat.

The Four Courts

Dublin City

A Dominican friary was on this site in the Middle Ages, and from the 16th century it was occupied by the King's Inns. In 1776, the architect Thomas Cooley undertook the construction of the Public Record Office there, but in 1785 it was decided to alter and increase the buildings in order to house the Four Courts (King's Bench, Chancery, Exchequer, and Common Pleas). The contract was given to James Gandon, a London architect who had already designed the Custom House in·Dublin. Gandon's buildings, completed in 1802, are dominated by a massive dome, and the front entrance is dramatised by six great pillars. The central statue on the pediment is of Moses, with Justice and Mercy on either side behind, and Wisdom and Authority on the corners of the roof. All of these statues were the work of Edward Smyth in 1792.

Beneath the dome is a large rotunda, with the courts radiating from it, each being entered through a pair of Corinthian columns. Other buildings, such as the Law Library, the Land Registry, and the new Public Record Office, were added later. In April 1922, the buildings were occupied by forces opposed to the treaty which had recently been negotiated with the British Government. The Civil War followed, and on June 28 the buildings were attacked by the official Free State forces. After fierce shelling, followed by hand-to-hand fighting, the buildings were captured within a few days. The fighting had caused extensive damage, and the buildings were not fully repaired until 1932. The Four Courts now function as the focal centre of the Irish judicial system.

Fore Monastic Site

County Westmeath

St. Féichín founded a monastery at this place, called in Irish *Fobhar* ('spring'), in the mid-7th century. He was famous not only for his sanctity, but also for his independence of mind. On one occasion, when the High-King Domhnall refused a request by him, it is said that Féichín fasted against that ruler, bringing snow-drifts to the kingdom and a fiery sword between him and his queen. The oldest building on the site, a rectangular church, postdates the death of Féichín in 665 AD. It has high pitched gables and a doorway with a massive lintel, inscribed with a cross. The de Lacy family founded a Benedictine priory at Fore, dedicated to Féichín and the Norman saint, Taurin, in the beginning of the 13th century. The nave and chancel of the original priory survive, but the castellated towers and the claustral buildings, with a fine arcade, date from the 15th century. Among the other remains are those of the priory pigeon-house and of a mediaeval church dedicated to St. Mary.

The atmosphere of the whole place, situated between hills and with its varying monastic buildings, is unusually peaceful and inspiring. Popular tradition claims that, due to the miraculous power of St. Féichín, there are 'seven wonders of Fore': an edifice constructed over a bog, a stream flowing uphill, the water of the well which will not boil, a tree the timber of which will not burn, a mill without a mill-stream, the image of an anchorite in stone, and the great stone lintel raised by an angel over the door of the ancient church. Today visitors hang strips of clothing of dead loved-ones on a shrub that is said to be dead but still yields foliage, in the hope that the deceased may enjoy eternal life.

Kilkea Castle

County Kildare

The Norman Viceroy, Hugh de Lacy, erected a stronghold of motte and bailey for Walter de Riddlesford in the year 1180, close to the early Christian site known as *Cill Chae* ('the church near the pathway'). When Emelina, the grand-daughter of Riddlesford, married Maurice Fitzgerald, 3rd Baron of Offaly, the new occupant decided to build a castle there, as well as a church for his family. Gerald, the son of Maurice and Emelina, died without issue in 1287, and the castle passed into the possession of the main line of the Fitzgerald family, the Earls of Kildare. The native Irish returned and took Kilkea in 1413, but they were defeated in a pitched battle nearby.

The Kildare Geraldines lost Kilkea, along with all their own possessions, in their failed rebellion of 1534. Eighteen years later, however, Gerald Fitzgerald, son of the executed earl, was installed as 11th Earl of Kildare. Enjoying the trust of the English authorities, he was an intelligent and efficient manager, repairing the castle and making the adjacent village one of the most important market-towns in Leinster. Folklore claims that he dabbled in the occult, conjuring up spirits and carrying out experiments in a secret room in the castle. After his death in 1585, Kilkea continued to be the main residence of the Kildare family until 1738. The castle was suspected of being a hiding place of the rebel leader, Lord Edward Fitzgerald, in 1798, and accordingly was plundered and occupied by the Redcoats. It was restored, with an extra storey added, by the Duke of Leinster in 1849-1853, and is today a luxury hotel.

MUNSTER

Drombeg Stone Circle

Poulnabrone Dolmen

County Clare

This is a striking example of the remains of a portal-tomb, of which there are many in Ireland. It dates from around 2,700 BC. In its original state, a portal-tomb consisted of a single chamber enclosed by large upright stones, with a large cap-stone laid on top of the uprights to form a roof. The cap-stone sloped downwards towards the back of the chamber. After a burial, the whole structure was sealed by smaller stones. When denuded by long centuries of weather and men seeking stones for less solemn buildings, the portal-tombs have the appearance of altars or great tables, adding to the mystery and mystique of the landscape.

The portal-tombs have been given many names, such as dolmens, cromlechs, and 'giant's graves'. In folk legend, such a structure is imaginatively called a *leaba* ('bed') of Diarmaid and Gráinne. This reflects the old romantic tale of how the maiden Gráinne was betrothed to Fionn Mac Cumhaill, but Fionn was by then an old man and she preferred the dashing young hero Diarmaid. The young lovers eloped and, being pursued throughout Ireland by Fionn and his men, they slept on top of these dolmens so that Diarmaid could fight off attackers from a favourable position on top of the capstone. It was also believed that a childless woman will conceive if she spends the night with her husband on such a 'bed'.

The Gallarus Oratory

County Kerry

Situated on a hillside slope in the west of the Dingle Peninsula, this boat-shaped oratory stands within a large stone-walled enclosure. Almost seven metres in length and six metres in breadth, the walls of the oratory are over a metre thick and are of sandstone. It has a corbelled vault, a lintelled doorway in the west gable, and a round-headed window in the east gable. On one side of it lies a bed of stones, on which stands a cross-slab of early date with an inscribed dedication to one 'Colum mac Dinet'.

The construction date for the Gallarus oratory is unclear – it may be as early as the 8th century or as late as the 12th century. It is the only perfect example of a boat-shaped building to survive in Ireland, and it is significant that it is situated in an area with a long tradition of seafaring. Another oratory nearby is in fact dedicated to the famous 6th-century saint, Brendan the Navigator. Towering over the area is Mount Brandon (*Cnoc Bhréanainn*), which takes its name from the saint, and Brendan himself was a native of the area. A local legend tells of how he once celebrated Mass on the mountain, but absent-mindedly left his missal in his oratory. So great was the assembled crowd, however, that nobody needed to move in order to collect the book – it was passed on from hand to hand all the seven-kilometre distance from the oratory to the mountain-top!

This great eminence, rising commandingly over the 'Golden Vale' of Munster, was the royal seat of the sept called Eoghanacht ('people of the yew'), which from the 4th century onwards dominated the southern half of Ireland. The origin myth of the Eoghanacht recalled how their ancestor, Conall Corc, came from Britain with his wife and three sons. They went astray in a snowstorm, through which only this massive rock could be discerned. Finding their way to it, they lit a fire at a yew-tree there. On the same night, a druid dreamed that whoever lit such a fire on the rock would be king of all Munster. The local people rushed to the place and, finding Conall there with his fire, they gave homage to the surprised stranger.

Christianity came early to the Rock of Cashel, and it was even claimed that St. Patrick himself had visited the place and baptised an Eoghanacht king, Aonghus, there. The ecclesiastical importance of the site was greatly enhanced by the rule in the 9th century of the scholar Cormac Mac Cuileannáin, reputed to have been simultaneously King of Munster and Bishop of Cashel. The surviving ecclesiastical buildings are, however, of much later date. The round tower – nearly 28 metres high – is the earliest of these; followed by the richly decorated Romanesque chapel, which was completed in 1134 by another king, Cormac Mac Cárthaigh. A cathedral was constructed on the site in 1169, but it was replaced about a century later by the present cathedral with its massive tower. Finally, a castle was constructed at the western part of this cathedral in the early 15th century by Archbishop Risteard Ó hEidhin.

The Rock of Cashel
County Tipperary

King John's Castle
Limerick City

The river Shannon briefly separates into two streams, making a small 'island' which was anciently known as *Inis Ibhdon*. This was where Norse raiders settled in 922 AD, and from which they gradually gained control of the surrounding 'bare marsh' (*Luimneach*, i.e. Limerick). Their power was broken within a few generations, and the area returned to Irish rule. Following on the Norman conquest, King Henry II toyed for a while with the idea of appointing his teenage son, John 'Lackland', as King of Ireland, and with this purpose sent him to acquaint himself with the country in 1177. John became captivated with the beauty of Limerick, and planned to build a castle there, a project which was enhanced twenty years later when John got a charter for the place from his brother, King Richard Lionheart. He began immediately to make grants of lands at Limerick to his friends.

John succeeded Richard as king and, when in 1210 he again visited Ireland, the castle was already completed, as well as a new bridge of fourteen arches leading from it directly across the Shannon. The core of Limerick City, the ancient *Inis Ibhdon*, now became known simply as 'King John's Island', and the castle stood there as a spectacular example of Norman architecture. Roughly rectangular in shape, it had massive walls with a tall defensive tower at each of the four corners. The scene of many battles down through the ages, in 1691 it witnessed the surrender of the Jacobite leader Patrick Sarsfield to the Williamite forces. The terms are said to have been signed atop the Treaty Stone, which is located nearby.

Clock Gate, Youghal

County Cork

In the early 13th century, one of the leading Norman families, the Fitzgeralds, built a town just west of the Blackwater estuary, at a place known as *Eochaill* ('yew-wood', anglicised as Youghal). There, in 1224, they established the first Franciscan friary in Ireland, and gradually added other abbeys and convents. The leading sept of these Fitzgeralds were later titled Earls of Desmond, and they ruled most of Munster in the manner of Gaelic kings. Always in touch with Continental affairs, Youghal was an important seaport for them and was one of their principal residences. Thomas Fitzgerald, the 7th Earl, established a college of learning there, based on Continental models, in 1464.

The next hundred years saw incessant pressure by the English on the Fitzgeralds, and the execution of several of their leaders. Seething resentment broke out in 1579 into a great rebellion led by Gerald, the 14th Earl. His first and major success was to retake Youghal, which had been garrisoned with a strong English force, but the rebellion collapsed and he himself was slain in 1583. Youghal was then given to Sir Walter Raleigh who, according to folklore, planted the first potatoes in Ireland in his garden there. Part of the mediaeval wall of the town, with towers, survives. A great iron gate separated the upper and lower parts of Youghal and, in 1777, it was replaced by the Clock Gate, the work of the architect William Meade. The building was used as a prison until 1837, and among those held there were several patriots awaiting execution after the Rising of 1798. It now serves as a genealogical research centre.

Drombeg Stone Circle

County Cork

Stone circles, containing the sacred within an invariable design, must have served several ritual purposes. Most of them were constructed in the early Bronze Age. Three kilometres east of the fishing village of Glandore in west Cork, in the townland of *Drom Beag* ('little hillock'), is a fine example, nine metres in diameter. It consists of seventeen great boulders, the two largest almost three metres in height, and one having an oval cup and other markings on it. At the centre of the circle was a flat stone, which covered a burial cyst containing the bones of a youth as well as cremation ashes in a simple urn. On a line from the entrance to the axial stone, this stone circle can be seen to be orientated towards the midwinter sunset.

Just 45 metres away, to the west, is an ancient open-air cooking-place. There are remains of two circular stone huts there, and the actual cooking site consisted of a rectangular trough, lined with flat stones, a well, and a hearth. Such a site, known as a *fulacht fiadh*, is of a type common in different parts of Ireland. The method of cooking was to fill the trough with water and bring the water to the boil by burning stones red-hot and placing them in the pit. Meat, wrapped in straw, was then placed in the water to be cooked. Carbonated dating shows that this *fulacht fiadh* was in use in the 5th and 6th centuries AD. The stone circle itself is much earlier, but the cooking nearby suggests that some social activity continued there for a long time.

Skellig Michael
County Kerry

Thirteen kilometres off the coast of the Iveragh Peninsula in south-west Kerry a bleak, towering island stands in the face of the wild Atlantic. Sixteen hectares in area, it has twin peaks, rising to 218 metres and 198 metres respectively above sea level. On a rock ledge about 170 metres high are the well-preserved remains of a monastic settlement, which can be reached by ascending pathways of neatly hewn steps. The settlement consists of the ruins of a church, two corbelled oratories, six stone 'beehive' dwellings, two wells, some stone-crosses and cross-slabs, and a small cemetery.

The settlement is associated with St. Fionnán, who lived in the 7th century. Remains of meagre gardens, fashioned by the monks with clay gathered from the rock crevices, illustrate how stern living conditions were on the island for the anchorite community who lived there for four centuries. In the Middle Ages, St. Michael was taken as patron of churches at lofty and desolate locations. Since such churches had to contend with tumultuous storms and sea, their struggle for survival was seen in terms of that of the Archangel against Lucifer. This rocky island in the Atlantic – the most desolate of all sacred settlements – was therefore given the name *Sceilg Mhichíl* ('the rock of Michael'). A pilgrimage to Skellig Michael was a particularly strict penitential exercise. Pilgrims would do the Stations of the Cross from the landing-place to the monastery, and sometimes would climb up the precipitous cliff to the highest peak above. There, they would kiss a cross, carved near the point of a narrow rock projecting perilously over the sea.

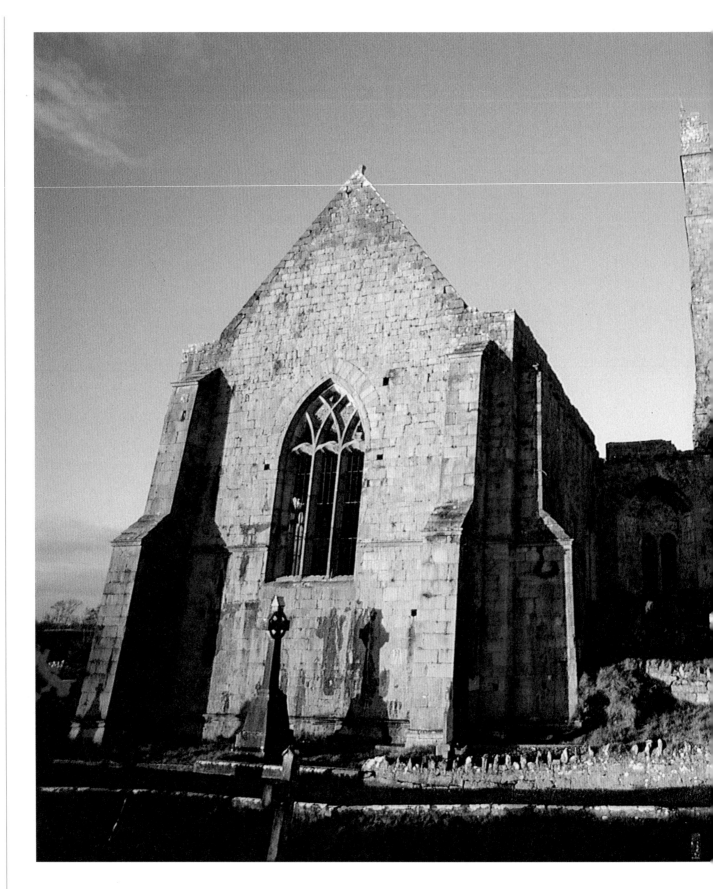

Quin Abbey
County Clare

Nine kilometres east of the present town of Ennis, at a place called *Cuinche* (an eponym anglicised as Quin), a castle was built in 1278 by the Norman leader, Thomas de Clare. Descendant of the famous 'Strongbow', Thomas seized much of north Munster but, a few months after his death in 1287, his castle was destroyed in the Irish resurgence. In 1402, the local chieftain, Síoda Cam Mac Conmara, decided to establish a Franciscan abbey on the site, but most of the building was not carried out until thirty years later. Remains of the old castle were utilised in the building, three of its walls and three of its four corner towers being incorporated into the new friary. The Mac Conmara sept had a strong devotion to Quin, and many generations of their leaders were interred in tombs there.

The ruins give a good insight into the architecture and layout of a mediaeval friary. Nave and chancel are divided by an elegant tower, and the cloister is in particularly good condition – its sharply arched arcades and buttressed walls giving it a striking aesthetic effect. The friary was suppressed during the campaign of Henry VIII against the monasteries in 1541, and the building was converted into an English army barracks, but repairs were carried out in 1604 by local families and the Franciscans were officially re-installed in 1626. Driven out again by the Cromwellians in 1651, they remained covertly in the district, considered by the people the rightful possessors of Quin. Their last member, Fr. John Hogan, died in 1820 at eighty-two years of age, and his tomb stands in the cloister.

Holy Cross Abbey
County Tipperary

Early in the 12th century, Pope Paschal II presented 'a fragment of the True Cross' to Muircheartach Ó Briain, one of the most powerful men in Ireland at the time. To preserve this relic, a little stone church was constructed on the eastern bank of the river Suir, within the territory of Muircheartach's mother. Then, in or about the year 1180, his grand-nephew, Dónall Mór Ó Briain, decided to replace that church with a great Cistercian abbey. Dónall was a great founder and endower of churches, but he was also a stern warrior and drove the Norman invaders from his territory.

The new building was called simply *Mainistir na Croiche Naofa* (Holy Cross Abbey), and it was quadrangular in shape, with the cloister on the southern side in order to catch the sunlight. After the death of Dónall Mór in 1194, the whole area was taken over by the Normans, but the monks were confirmed in their title by King John. Later on, the abbey came under the protection of the powerful Butler family, Earls of Ormond, and at the beginning of the 15th century a great project of rebuilding began. Most of the modern structure dates from this period, including the elaborate windows and the fine stone carvings. A folk tradition claims that Cearbhall Ó Dálaigh, a celebrated poet and artisan, worked on the rebuilding and left a carving of a cat with two tails as his trademark there. Due to the Butler protection, the abbey survived the general closure of monasteries by Henry VIII, and a small number of monks clung on there until the 18th century.

Lough Gur
County Limerick

People were in this small hilly area in the middle of the flat and fertile plain of Munster at least since the 4th millennium BC, and the whole surroundings are rich in megalithic tombs, standing stones, stone circles, ancient fields and roads, timber hut sites, and stone-forts. There is a horse-shoe-shaped lake, on the northern side of which is the massive hill called Knockfennell, where remains of prehistoric animals such as elk and brown bear have been found; and to its east – within the curve of the 'horse-shoe' – is the smaller and more smooth-shaped hill of Knockadoon. There is only one natural island on the lake, with evidence of early habitation, but two other 'islands' by the shore were constructed as ancient lake-dwellings called crannóga. The lake got its name (*Loch Gair*) from a local sept called anciently 'the men of Gar'.

From the 13th century onwards, Lough Gur was a centre of the Earls of Desmond, who built the Black Castle on the southern side of Knockadoon. Bourchier's Castle was later built on the northern side of that hill. There are many legends in the locality concerning the celebrated 3rd Earl, Gerald Fitzgerald, known as *Gearóid Iarla*, who is said not to have died but to have been enchanted. The island bears his name (*Oileán Ghearóid*), and the tradition is that he lives on with a ghostly army, waiting to return, in the Red Cellar Cave in the heart of Knockfennell. Every Midsummer Night he rides once around the lake on a white stallion. When the silver shoes of the stallion are worn out, *Gearóid Iarla* will return.

Bull Rock

County Kerry

The ancient Celts believed that the spirits of the dead departed with the setting sun. In the 1st century AD, Plutarch reports that a Greek traveller had told him of a belief in Britain that ghostly boats brought the dead to a western island and that, on arrival, the names of those who disembarked were called out by a mysterious voice. The belief was in Ireland too, where it was claimed that a divine personage called Donn ('the dark one') presided over the dead on a small island off the south-west coast.

This is the desolate rock known as *Teach Duinn* ('the House of Donn'), which rises to over 85 metres above sea level and has a very unusual formation, being in effect a natural archway under which the sea flows with tremendous force. It is called in English 'Bull Rock', and lies to the west of Dursey Island, in all ten kilometres from the point of the Beara Peninsula, being the most westerly piece of land in all that area. A pre-Christian prayer in Irish has Donn stating: 'To me, to my house, you shall all come after your deaths!' This strange and solitary rock replicated the shape of the ancient burial dolmens. It was therefore a portal to the unknown resting place of the dead, an idea which can easily impress itself on the observer from the shore line who sees the last rays of the setting sun pierce through it. Something of a change in the role of Bull Rock occurred with the location there since 1889 of a very important lighthouse.

The Paps of Danu

County Kerry

The gods of the Irish Celts were known as *Tuatha Dé Danann* ('people of the goddess Danu'). The name of that goddess as a mother figure was known also to the Celts of Britain, and there is little doubt but that her cult is very ancient. She has, indeed, cognates in the names of goddesses in other Indo-European traditions, such as the Indic Dánu and the Greek Danaë. It would appear to have been a name given in particular to water-deities, as evidenced by many European river-names. Rivers are, of course, responsible for the fertility of the soil, and Irish tradition tended to place Danu in the role of earth-goddess.

The earth nourishes and provides food for the people and so – just as they viewed the sun as the father-god – the ancient Irish thought of the earth as the divine mother. This is reflected by two mounds at the royal centre of Tara in County Meath, which were known as 'the paps of the great queen'. Even more graphic was the tradition in west Munster, where the name Danu was often confused with another word, *anae*, meaning 'wealth'. The protective goddess was totally identified with the land in the case of the twin peaks about 15 kilometres east of the Lakes of Killarney. These are of near equal height, each rising to a height of almost 700 metres, and are within a kilometre of each other. They are shaped astonishingly like the breasts of a woman, and therefore have been known from time immemorial as *Dá Chích Dhanann* ('the two paps of Danu').

Ogham Stone
Dunloe, County Kerry

The ancient Continental Celts had a god called Ogmios, who personified eloquence and whose tongue was joined by mystical chains to the ears of human listeners. In Irish, he was called Oghma, being described as 'one most knowledgeable in speech and in poetry'. When knowledge of the Latin alphabet reached Ireland in or about the 3rd century AD, a special system of representing the letters was developed and – out of respect for the deity Oghma – this system of writing was called *ogham*. In place of the Latin orthography, a special system of notches for the vowels and grooves for the consonants was used.

Early accounts refer to rhetorics and charms being written in ogham on timber, and even to poets using the script to write down legendary stories on tablets. Almost all the surviving evidence for the script, however, relates to memorial inscriptions for the dead. These inscriptions were written on upright stones which marked the burials of important leaders. The *ogham* stones are especially plentiful in southern parts of Ireland, but some are found also in areas settled by the Irish in Wales, the Isle of Man, and Scotland. The form of the Irish language found in the inscriptions is older than that found in Irish literature proper, which began to be written on vellum from the 6th century onwards. The *ogham* writing was popularly thought to contain magical power, and this may indeed have been the attitude of those who first expressed the spoken words of the Irish language in this way over a millennium and a half ago.

Round Tower

Ardmore, County Waterford

Déaglán ('little deacon') was one of the earliest monks in Ireland, dating perhaps to the end of the 5th century AD. He belonged to the Waterford area and founded a celebrated monastery at Ardmore. Biographical accounts of him, however, date to several centuries later. In these, he is described as banishing a plague through his miraculous power, having a stag draw his chariot, and restoring both people and animals to life. One of the most phantastic stories tells of a visit made by him to Rome, where he was presented with a beautiful little bell. When sailing home from Wales to Ireland, his servant inadvertently left the bell on a rock, but in answer to Déaglán's prayer the rock floated of its own accord across the sea to Ardmore. It still lies on the strand there, resting on two other rocks, and people squeeze through the narrow passage underneath it to rid themselves of ailments.

Most of the ecclesiastical remains on the site belong to the Middle Ages, but some inscribed standing stones from the early period remain, as well as the grave of the saint. The Round Tower, from the 12th century, is one of the finest and best-preserved in Ireland. It is over 29 metres high and 5 metres in diameter, and has four storeys, each clearly marked on the outside. There are several windows, and the round-headed door is well above ground level. In the interior is a series of heads carved from projecting stones. The capstone of the tower fell in the 1860s and has been replaced by a modern construction with a cross on top.

ULSTER

Navan Fort

Near the mouth of Lough Foyle, St. Columba founded a monastery in the 6th century at a 'little wood', *Doire*. Under the patronage of the Mac Lochlainn dynasty in the 12th century, the settlement around the monastery grew into a strong trading port. It was captured by an English army under Sir Henry Docwra in 1600 and, when the Plantation of Ulster got under way, King James I granted a charter to twelve companies from London to found a new city there. The name of the place was changed from Derry to Londonderry, and the new lay-out was modelled on that of the French town Vitry-le-François. A strong wall encompassing it, over six metres high and two metres thick, was completed in 1618. Thirty years later, when occupied by a Cromwellian army, the city was besieged by the Royalists, but was relieved by the Irish army of Eoghan Rua Ó Néill.

Supporting the cause of William of Orange, thirteen apprentices shut the gates of the city against the Earl of Antrim and his Scottish soldiers in December 1688. King James II himself arrived to lay siege to Derry in the following April but, despite the desertion of their military commander, Colonel Lundy, the Williamite defenders stood firm under the leadership of the Reverend George Walker. In the beginning of July the besiegers constructed a boom across the river Foyle to prevent relief ships from reaching the city. Three weeks later, however, the boom was broken by a ship called the 'Mountjoy'. Lacking big guns and weakened by heavy losses, the Jacobite army withdrew.

The Fortified Walls of Derry

Derry City

Giant's Causeway
County Antrim

Situated on the north Antrim coast, on the western side of Benbane Head, this remarkable geological formation was brought about millions of years ago by the cooling of lava into enormous quantities of basalt. The splitting rock has resulted in thousands of upright columns of differing size, with the appearance of having been wedged against each other. The amount of sides on these columns varies between three and nine. Irregular in height, and stretching for some distance out into the sea from under huge cliffs, these basalt columns are difficult to walk on and hence were given the name *Clochán an Aifir* ('stepping-stones of penance').

In Victorian times, this was a favourite place for sight-seeing by visitors, who did not hesitate to use their imagination, calling it 'the Giant's Causeway' as if it had been deliberately placed there by some such gigantic personage. Noticing the variation in the shape of sections, they gave specific names to these, such as 'the Amphitheatre', 'the Giant's Chair', 'the Giant's Organ', 'Lord Antrim's Parlour', and 'the Lady's Fan'. Drawing on the ancient lore of Fionn Mac Cumhaill – opponent of giants and sometimes himself portrayed as a giant – some have humorously considered the whole formation as the remains of a passage which that hero had constructed so as to travel dryshod from Ireland to Scotland! Coincidentally, modern geologists have shown that the volcanic rift which caused the formation did in fact extend from the coast of Antrim to the Isle of Skye in Scotland.

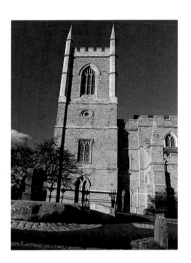

Downpatrick Cathedral

County Down

This stately cathedral, dating to the late 18th and early 19th centuries, is built on the ruins of a mediaeval Benedictine abbey, which in turn replaced an earlier church at the site of a hill-fort called Dún Leathghlaise. According to legend, St. Patrick was the founder of that church, and a major part of the saint's missionary activity was indeed carried out in the surrounding area. A 7th-century biographer claims that, after his death, Patrick's body was placed in a cart drawn by untamed oxen, and guided by the will of God the oxen brought the corpse to this place. Although many scholars doubt that this was the location of his last resting place, the tradition was so strong in the Middle Ages that the place was renamed Dún Phádraig ('the fortress of Patrick').

The legend of Downpatrick grew, and it was claimed that the relics of not only Patrick, but also of the other two famous saints of Ireland, Brigid and Columba, were discovered there. It is a historical fact that in 825 AD the Vikings raided the island monastery of Iona off the Scottish coast and plundered the grave of Columba. This led to a story of how these raiders, angered at finding nothing of value, had flung the coffin of Columba into the sea. The coffin, it was said, floated over the sea to Ireland and, on being discovered on the coast of County Down, was brought for reburial to Downpatrick. When it reached the cemetery there, the coffins of Patrick and Brigid moved apart so as to allow room for Columba to be buried between them!

Navan Fort
County Armagh

A large enclosure was erected on this hill-top site at the beginning of the 1st century BC. Within the enclosure were four concentric rings of oak posts. Towards the centre was a circle of timber uprights, within which again was a large post stuck into a hole. Soon after, the inner structure was filled with limestone blocks and the walling burned, and finally it was sealed by covering it over with sods. There is no doubting that this was a sacred site, but opinion is divided as to whether its deliberate destruction was a ritual act or an act of war.

The ancient Celtic name of the site was *Isomnis* (probably meaning 'strong oaks'), which developed in Irish into *an Eamhain* (hence the anglicised form 'Navan'). The early Ulstermen considered it the central point of their kingship, calling it *Eamhain Mhacha* ('Navan of the Plain'), which was in time misunderstood to mean 'Navan of Macha'. Accordingly, Macha was taken to be a nickname of the *Mór-Ríoghain* ('great queen'), the Irish version of the goddess of sovereignty. This goddess was often associated with horses, and so the origin-legend of Navan has a lady called Macha winning a race against horses at the site. Other legends claim that Macha directed the building of the fort, one stating that she sat on the hill and planned the perimeter of the mound with a pin from her mantle. The pin stretched further eastwards in front of her than behind her to the west, causing the mound to be uneven! In mediaeval epic, Navan Fort was regarded as the headquarters of the ancient Ulster heroes.

Figures on Boa Island

County Fermanagh

At the western end of Boa Island (*Inis Badhbha*) on Lower Lough Erne is an ancient churchyard which contains these extraordinary figures engraved in a stone, three-quarters of a metre in height. They are twin figures, set back to back, and have enormous heads with large eyes, gaping mouths, and pointed chins. Underneath each head are what have often been interpreted as tiny crossed arms, but which were probably intended by the sculptor to represent crossed legs in a squatting pose. This sculpture seems to have always been at its present location, but the effigy stone beside it has been brought here from Lusty More Island nearby.

Opinions differ as to the age of these sculpted figures, some regarding them as belonging to the pre-Christian period and others placing them as late as the 7th century AD. Somewhat similar figures are on White Island, also on Lough Erne, and these are clearly ecclesiastical, representing monks and saints. The truth may be that the Boa Island figures were sculpted by Christians to represent pre-Christian personages, probably druids who were being displaced by the monks, and that they were therefore intended as caricatures. Their dwarf-like appearance is not complimentary, and their squatting posture suggests an involuntary surrender to the miraculous power of Christian clerics. Their situation on the 'island of the *Badhbh*' is of interest, as this was a name commonly given to the Celtic land-goddess. The island would seem to have been a sacred place to the druids, and its conversion to Christianity would therefore have been considered a triumph worthy of a memorial.

Grianán Ailigh

County Donegal

The celebrated Niall 'of the Nine Hostages' was king of Tara in the 5th century AD, and in a general extension of his power three of his sons pushed to the north-west of Ireland and set up kingdoms for themselves in that region. One of these sons was Eoghan, who founded the kingdom of Aileach and began the construction of a massive stone fort on a small mountain west of the river Foyle, immediately opposite where Derry City now stands. Known as 'the palace of Aileach', the fort is circular, with a diameter of nearly 24 metres. The walls are over 5 metres high and 4 metres thick, and have three terraces reached by steps. The entrance, on the eastern side, is narrow. Remains of three earthen banks surrounding the Grianán still remain, the total area enclosed by them being 1.6 hectares.

The kings of Aileach were the northern O'Neills, and for several generations they shared the High-Kingship of Ireland alternately with the southern O'Neills of Tara. Their most famous king was Niall Frasach (717-778), celebrated for his moderation, holiness, and wise judgements. His ambitious descendant, Muircheartach 'of the Leather Cloaks', made a conquering circuit of Ireland in 941 AD and returned to the Grianán with many hostages. In 1088 the King of Aileach, Dónall Mac Lochlainn, in a raid on Munster destroyed the royal seat of the O'Briens at Kincora in County Clare, and in a revenge attack thirteen years later Muircheartach Ó Briain demolished the Grianán. It remained in ruins until restored by Dr. Bernard of Derry in 1870.

Stormont Castle

Belfast

In the British general election held at the end of 1918, the Sinn Féin party took the overwhelming majority of seats in Ireland, and its elected representatives set up an independent Irish *Dáil* ('parliament'). The British Government refused to accept this, and within a few months the situation had deteriorated into war. As the fighting continued, the Government of Ireland Act was passed by Westminster in 1920, which partitioned the country, creating a new state comprising the six north-eastern counties, where there was a pro-British majority. This was quickly accepted by the Unionists, and the British Government made a gift of a magnificent new building to the new parliament of Northern Ireland. This, Stormont Castle, was designed in Neo-Classical style by Sir Arnold Thornby, and was opened by King George V in 1921.

Situated in 120 hectares of parkland, and with a climbing processional entrance over 1,000 metres long, Stormont was completed by 1932. In front of the building is a statue of the Unionist leader, Lord Edward Carson, by L. S. Merrifield. The subsequent history of the Stormont parliament was controversial, with the in-built Unionist majority determined to perpetuate their numerical advantage and social dominance. Continuing Nationalist resentment and sporadic violence broke out in 1969 into a sustained guerrilla campaign by the IRA (Irish Republican Army), which caused the British Government to prorogue the parliament in 1972 and introduce direct rule from Westminster. Twenty-five years later a ceasefire ended the longest war in Irish history, and a new system of government was introduced, according to which Unionists and Nationalists shared power.

Dunluce Castle

County Antrim

On the north coast of Antrim is a basalt rock – 38 metres high – cut off from the mainland by a deep chasm. The encroaching sea has even cut a tunnel through the rock itself. Desolate though this rock is, overhanging the sea, it was occupied since the late Iron Age, forming a promontory fort called *Dún Lis* ('the fortress of the enclosure'). The Vikings were there in the Middle Ages, and the castle was built in the 13th century by the Normans. It later passed into the hands of the local Gaelic chieftains, the MacQuillans. By marriage with them, the celebrated Somhairle Buí, chieftain of the MacDonnells, was in possession by 1560. He salvaged cannon from the wreck of an Armada ship in 1588 and reinforced the castle with them. His son Randal was created Earl of Antrim in 1620.

During a feast there in 1629, part of the structure collapsed into the sea, and many of the servants were drowned. The south wall of the original castle, facing the land, survives, as do two of the original towers, some turrets, and broken façades. Other remains, including the gatehouse and stone bridge, date from the early 17th century. According to legend, the great Highland warrior of the MacDonnell clan, Alasdair Mac Colla, was invited to a feast there in 1641 when the castle was in the control of the English army. It was intended to arrest him, but when told to surrender his sword he refused, saying that it was in the best hand in Ireland or Scotland. When asked what was the second best hand, he changed the sword into his other hand, and left unmolested!

Picture Credits

The publishers are grateful to Brian Kelly, photographer and proprietor of BSK Photo Library, Dublin, for assembling such a fine collection of photographs, and to the photographers and institutions who made them available for this book, as follows:

Page 1: Don Sutton; 2-3, 4-5, 6-7: Michael Diggin; 9: Fabian Lee; 10: Brian Kelly; 12-13 Charles Bateman; 14-15: Robert Vance; 16-17: Brian Kelly; 18-19: left, Charles Bateman, right, Don Sutton; 20-21: Brian Kelly; 22-23: Charles Bateman; 24-25: left, Andrew Hill, right, Don Sutton; 26-27: Andrew Hill; 28-29: left, Don Sutton, right, Brian Kelly; 30-31: Brian Kelly; 32-33: left, Brian Kelly, right, Philip Clooney; 34-35: Brian Kelly; 36-37: left, Brian Kelly, right, Tom Cleary; 38-39: left, BSK Photo Library, right, Brian Kelly; 40-41: left, Brian Kelly, right, Andrew Hill; 42-43: Trinity College; 44-45: Michael Diggin; 46-47: BSK Photo Library; 48-49: Brian Kelly; 50-51: left, Charles Bateman, right, Don Sutton; 52-53: Michael Diggin; 54-55: left, Brian Kelly, right, Don Sutton; 56-57: Don Sutton; 58-59, 60-61, 62-63: National Museum of Ireland; 64-65, 66-67, 68-69, 70-71: Brian Kelly; 72-73: National Museum of Ireland; 74-75: Brian Kelly; 76-77: National Museum of Ireland; 78-79: left, Tom Cleary, right, Michael Diggin; 80-81: Royal Irish Academy; 82-83: Michael Diggin; 84-85: Brian Kelly; 86-87: Don Sutton; 88-89, 90-91: Brian Kelly; 92-93: John Eagle; 94-95: left, Don Sutton, right, Brian Cross; 96-97: Michael Diggin; 98-99: left, Don Sutton, right, Michael Diggin; 100-101: left, Michael Diggin, right, Brian Cross; 102-103: left, John Eagle, right, Michael Diggin; 104-105: John Eagle; 106-107: left, Michael Diggin, right, John Eagle; 108-109: Brian Kelly; 110-111, 112-113: Michael Diggin; 114-115, 116-117: John Eagle; 118-119: Michael Diggin; 120-121: left, Don Sutton, right, Michael Diggin; 122-123, 124-125: Charles Bateman; 126-127: Brian Kelly; 128-129, 130-131: Charles Bateman; 132-133: Don Sutton; 134-135: Robert Vance; 136-137: Charles Bateman; 138-139, 140-141: Don Sutton.

Quin Abbey

Index

Leabharlanna Atha Cliath
RATHMINES LIBRARY
Invoice : 01/1400 Price IR£10.25
Title: Historic Ireland 5,00
Class: 941.5

Items should be returned on or before the last date
shown below. Items not already requested by other
borrowers may be renewed in person, in writing or by
telephone. To renew, please quote the number on the
barcode label. To renew online a PIN is required.
This can be requested at your local library.
Renew online @ **www.dublincitypubliclibraries.ie**
Fines charged for overdue items will include postage
incurred in recovery. Damage to or loss of items will
be charged to the borrower.

Leabharlanna Poiblí Chathair Bhaile Átha Cliath
Dublin City Public Libraries

 Rathmines Branch Tel. 4973539

Dublin City
Baile Átha Cliath

Date Due	Date Due	Date Due
24_03.14		
1 4 FEB 2019		